The New Chicken Cookbook

50 Quick and Simple Recipes for Every Day

Angelina Baker

Table of Contents

ORIENTAL CHICKEN TENDERS CURRIED PEANUT CHICKEN

- 1 c. soy sauce
- 1/3 c. sugar
- 4 tsp. vegetable oil
- 1 1/2 tsp. ground ginger
- 1 tsp. five spice powder
- 2 bunches green onion
- 16 chicken tenders (approx. 2 lbs.)

Blend soy sauce, sugar, oil, ginger and five spice powder in a large bowl until the sugar dissolves. Stir in green onions. Add chicken tenders to marinade. Turn to coat.

Cover chicken and refrigerate overnight. Preheat oven to 350 degrees.

Drain chicken RESERVING MARINADE. Arrange the chicken in dish and bake until brown and tender, while basting occasionally with marinade.

Another variation of the same recipe:

- 4 halves, skinned & boned chicken breasts
- 2 c. half & half
- 1 1/2 c. mayonnaise
- 3 tbsp. mango chutney
- 2 tbsp. dry sherry
- 1 tbsp. sherry vinegar
- 2 tbsp. plus 1 tsp. curry powder
- 1 tsp. turmeric
- 2 c. finely chopped salted roasted peanuts

Preheat oven to 350 degrees. Place chicken breasts in a shallow baking dish just large enough to hold them. Pour half and half over them and bake for 30 minutes. Let cool and cut in 1-inch cubes.

Process mayonnaise, chutney, sherry, vinegar, curry powder and turmeric in a blender or food processor.

Dip chicken pieces into the curry mayonnaise and roll in the chopped nuts. Refrigerate 30 minutes. Arrange on a serving plate with fancy toothpicks.

ORIENTAL CHICKEN WINGS

- 6 chicken wings
- 1 sm. clove garlic
- 1 scallion
- 1/4 c. soy sauce
- 2 tbsp. honey
- 2 tsp. rice-wine vinegar
- 1/2 tsp grated ginger
- 1/2 tsp. oriental sesame oil
- Pinch of cayenne
- 1 tsp. sesame seeds
- 1 tbsp. chopped fresh coriander or parsley

Remove wing tips and cut wings in half at the joint. Mince garlic and scallion. Combine soy sauce, honey, vinegar, garlic, ginger, oil and cayenne in a microwave safe dish.

Add wings and turn to coat. Marinate at least 30 minutes, turning twice. Put larger wings at the edge of the dish. Cover with plastic and vent. Microwave on high for 5 minutes.

Rotate plate and cook 5 minutes longer. Transfer wings to a serving plate. Return marinade to oven and cook, partially covered on high for 2 minutes.

Pour marinade over wings and turn to coat. Sprinkle with sesame seeds, scallion and coriander. 12 pieces.

APRICOT CHICKEN WINGS

- 1 pkg. Lipton onion soup
- 1 jar apricot preserves
- 1 bottle of clear Russian dressing
- 2 lbs. chicken wings

Bake chicken wings in oven at 350 degrees until tender (1 hour). Mix soup mix, preserves and Russian dressing.

Pour mixture over the chicken wings, coating each piece and serve hot.

CHICKEN WINGS

- 36 chicken wings
- 1 (5 oz.) bottle soy sauce
- 1 tsp. Dijon mustard
- 4 tbsp. brown sugar
- 1/2 tsp. garlic powder

Rinse chicken wings and pat dry. Mix soy sauce, mustard, brown sugar and garlic powder together. Marinate wings in mixture overnight (or about 6 hours). Bake wings on cookie sheet for about 1 hour at 375 degrees. Baste wings occasionally with sauce. Serves 9-12.

HOT-N-SPICY CHICKEN WINGS

- 5 lbs. bag chicken wings (drumettes)
- 12 fl. oz. Louisiana Pre Crystal Hot Sauce
- 1-2 sticks butter

Fry chicken wings until golden brown and drain on paper towel. Mix hot sauce and melted butter and pour into deep pan or crock pot.

Add chicken wings to sauce and heat thoroughly.

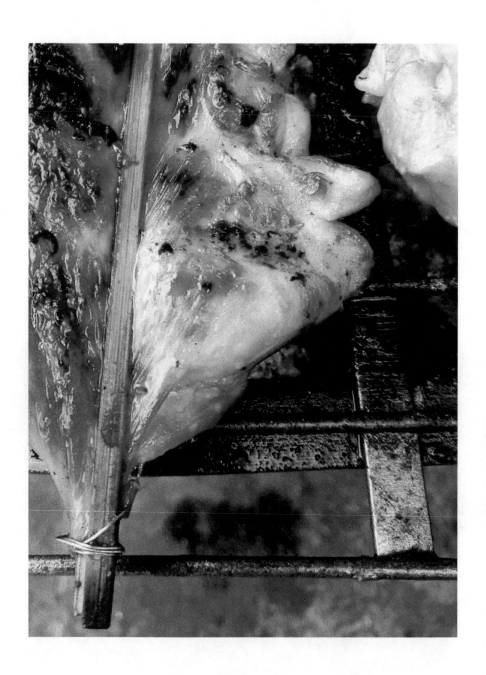

CHICKEN BITS

Debone 2 whole chicken breasts. Cut in bite-size pieces. Dip in melted butter. Roll in seasoned breadcrumbs (Italian seasoning with extra Parmesan cheese added).

Put on ungreased cookie sheet. Bake at 350 degrees for 30 minutes. Yields 36 bite-size.

SPICY CHICKEN WINGS

- 1 lg. can Parmesan cheese
- 2 tbsp. oregano
- 4 tbsp. parsley
- 1 tsp. salt
- 1 tsp. pepper
- 1 stick margarine
- 4-5 lbs. chicken wings

Line cookie sheet with aluminum foil. Melt margarine in small pan. Cut up chicken wings. Discard tips.

Mix all dry ingredients in bowl. Dunk chicken wings in margarine and roll in cheese mixture.

Place on cookie sheet. Bake in preheated 350-degree oven for 1 hour. Serve warm.

CHICKEN FRY ICED TEA

- 5 lbs. sugar
- 4 oz. plus 1 c. instant tea
- 1 gal. boiling water

Blend until sugar melts; let steep. Use 10-gallon container and add large block of ice and 7 1/2 to 8 gallons cold water. Then pour the strong tea solution into it slowly.

Stir well. Triple this recipe should serve 500.

CRISPY ORIENTAL CHICKEN WINGS (MICROWAVE)

- 1 1/2 lbs. chicken wings, disjointed
- 1 med. egg
- 1/2 c. soy sauce
- 2 tbsp. garlic powder
- 1/4 tsp. ginger powder
- 1 med. onion, finely diced
- 2 c. finely crushed corn flakes

Mix egg, soy sauce, garlic powder and ginger powder. Set aside. On wax paper, mix crushed corn flakes and diced onion. Dip each wing in soy sauce mixture, then roll in corn flakes and onion.

In glass baking dish, cover and cook wings on high (9) for 20 minutes, or until cooked. Remove covering halfway through cooking. Use 13"x9" baking dish.

Yield: 24 appetizers.

TERIYAKI CHICKEN WINGS

- 1/3 c. lemon juice
- 1/4 c. soy sauce
- 1/4 c. vegetable oil
- 3 tbsp. chili sauce
- 1 clove garlic, finely chopped
- 1/4 tsp. pepper
- 1/4 tsp. celery seed
- Dash of dry mustard
- 3 lb. chicken wings

MARINADE: Combine lemon juice, soy sauce, oil, chili sauce, garlic, pepper, celery seed and mustard. Stir well, set aside. Cut chicken wings at joint and remove wing tips. Place chicken in baking dish.

Pour marinade over chicken. Cover refrigerate at least 4 hours or overnight. Drain and place on broiler tray. Broil about 10 minutes each side with tray about 7 inches from heating element. Brush occasionally with marinade.

HOT CHICKEN WINGS

- Chicken wings
- 1/2 stick margarine
- 1 bottle Durkee hot sauce
- 2 tbsp. honey
- 10 shakes Tabasco
- 2 tsp. cayenne pepper (optional)

Deep fry wings for 20 minutes. Drain and dip and let set in sauce. Take out to dry and then serve.

HIDDEN VALLEY CHICKEN DRUMMIES

- 20 chicken drummies
- Good 1/4 c. butter, melted
- 1 tbsp. hot pepper sauce
- 2 tbsp. vinegar
- 2 pkgs. Hidden Valley dressing mix
- Paprika
- Celery sticks

Dip chicken in mixture of melted butter, pepper sauce and vinegar. Put in baking pan. Sprinkle with 1 package dry dressing mix.

Bake 30 minutes at 350 degrees or until browned. Sprinkle with paprika. Serve with celery sticks and prepared Hidden Valley dressing mix as dip.

MARINATED CHICKEN WINGS

- 2 doz. chicken wings
- 5 oz. bottle soy sauce
- 2 tbsp. brown sugar
- 1 tsp. Dijon mustard
- 1/2 tsp. garlic powder

Cut chicken wings in half. Marinate in remaining mixture for 1/2 hour. Bake at 350 degrees for 1 hour or until marinate is thick. Turn once. Serves 6 to 10.

COMMENT: May be frozen in marinade. Bake after defrosting.

GOLDEN CHICKEN NUGGETS

- 4 whole chicken breasts, skinned & deboned
- 1/2 c. unseasoned fine breadcrumbs
- 1/4 c. grated Parmesan cheese
- 1 tsp. salt
- 1 tsp. thyme (or 1/4 tsp. powdered thyme)
- 1 tsp. basil
- 1/2 c. butter, melted

Cut chicken into bite-size pieces. Mix dry ingredients. Dip chicken into butter, then into crumb mixture.

Bake on foil-lined cookie sheet at 400 degrees for 10 minutes. Serves 8 to 10.

MARINATED CHICKEN WINGS

- 1/2 c. soy sauce
- 1/2 c. honey
- 1 tsp. garlic powder
- 1 tsp. chili powder
- 2 lb. chicken wings with drum end cut at joint from wing, discard tips

Mix ingredients together and marinate cut-up wings overnight. Place wing parts in shallow baking pan and pour remaining liquid over them.

Bake for 1 hour at 325 degrees, turning on the 1/2 hour.

SWEET AND SOUR CHICKEN WINGS

- 2 1/2 lb. chicken wings with tips removed
- 1/3 c. Crisco
- 1/3 c. vinegar
- 1/2 c. firmly packed dark brown sugar
- 1 (12 oz.) can unsweetened pineapple juice
- 3/4 c. catsup
- 1 tbsp. soy sauce
- 1 tsp. prepared mustard
- 1/8 tsp. salt (optional)

Brown wings in hot Crisco, adding more, if necessary. Remove wings as they brown. Drain drippings from skillet. Add vinegar, sugar, juice, catsup, soy sauce, mustard, and salt to skillet. Bring to boil, stirring occasionally.

Simmer gently about 5 minutes. Add browned chicken wings. Cover skillet. Simmer 15 minutes. Turn wings and cook uncovered 15 minutes longer. Serve with rice. Makes 4 servings.

CHICKEN WINGS IN SOY SAUCE

- 24 chicken wings
- 1 c. soy sauce
- 3/4 c. chopped green onions with tops
- 1/3 c. sugar
- 4 tsp. salad oil
- 1 clove garlic, crushed
- 1 1/2 tsp. ground ginger

Halve the wings and throw away the tips. Blend soy sauce, onions, sugar, oil, garlic and ginger in a large bowl. Add the wings, cover and marinate for 30 minutes. Remove the wings and reserve the marinade. Place the chicken in a shallow pan and baste with the sauce.

Bake in 350-degree oven for 15 minutes and turn over, baste again and cook 15 more minutes. This may be made the day before and reserved in refrigerator, covered. Be sure to save some marinade to baste again when reheating in oven.

BUFFALO-STYLE CHICKEN WINGS

- 2 1/2 lb. (12-15) chicken wings
- 1/4 c. Durkee red hot sauce
- 1 stick (1/2 c.) melted butter or margarine
- Celery sticks
- Blue cheese dip

Split wings at joint and discard tips. Arrange on a rack in a roasting pan. Cover wing pieces with sauce on both sides. Bake at 425 degrees for 1 hour, turning halfway through cooking time.

Wings can be deep fried at 400 degrees for about 12 minutes and then dipped into the hot sauce until coated completely. Serve with celery and blue cheese dip.

CRISPY CASHEW CHICKEN (MADE IN WOK)

- 2 egg whites
- 1 1/4 c. finely chopped cashew nuts
- 2 whole chicken breasts, skinned, boned and thinly sliced
- 2c. peanut or vegetable oil
- 1/4 c. cornstarch
- 1 tsp. sugar
- 2 tsp. salt
- 1 1/2 tbsp. dry sherry

In small bowl, combine cornstarch, salt, sugar and sherry. In separate bowl, beat egg white lightly until just frothy. Gradually add cornstarch mixture. Stir gently until blended. Place chopped cashews on plate.

Dip chicken slices into egg mixture, then coat with cashews. Place on waxed paper. Pour oil into wok, place tempura rack onto wok, making sure rack is level and hooks rest securely on edge of wok.

Heat oil over medium to medium-high heat until it reaches 375 degrees. Drop 5 or 6 slices of chicken carefully into hot oil, using a slotted spoon. Fry until golden brown, about 2 to 3 minutes.

Remove from oil and place on tempura rack to drain and keep warm. Continue frying remaining chicken pieces. Makes about 32 appetizers.

CURRIED CHICKEN BALLS

- 2 (3 oz.) pkg. cream cheese, softened
- 2 tbsp. orange marmalade
- 2 tsp. curry powder
- 3/4 tsp. salt
- 1/4 tsp. pepper
- 3 c. finely minced cooked chicken
- 3 tbsp. minced green onion
- 3 tbsp. minced celery
- 1 c. finely chopped almonds, toasted

In a mixing bowl, combine first 5 ingredients. Beat until smooth. Stir in chicken, onion and celery. Shape into 1-inch balls; roll in almonds.

Cover and chill until firm (can refrigerate up to 2 days). Yield: about 5 dozen appetizers.

LIGHT CHICKEN SALAD

- 3/4 c. light mayonnaise
- 1/2 tsp. ginger
- 1/2 tsp. salt
- 3 c. cooked chicken
- 1 1/2 c. red seedless grapes
- 1 c. sliced celery
- 1/3 c. sliced green onion
- 1/2 c. broken walnuts

Combine mayonnaise, ginger and salt. Stir in chicken, grapes, celery, green onion and walnuts.

Makes 5 1/2 cups. Serve on lettuce leaf.

HOT CHICKEN SALAD

- 1 1/2 c. cooked chicken, diced
- 1 c. diced celery
- 3 diced boiled eggs
- 1/2 tsp. salt
- 1 sm. jar pimentos
- 2 tbsp. chopped green onions
- 1 1/2 c. breadcrumbs
- 1/2 c. slivered almonds
- 3 tbsp. lemon juice
- 3/4 c. mayonnaise
- 1 can cream of chicken soup
- 1 stick oleo

Mix everything together except breadcrumbs, and oleo. Butter casserole dish (10 x 12 inch). Put complete mixture in dish. Put breadcrumbs on top.

Melt butter and sprinkle over the breadcrumbs. Bake at 350 degrees for 30 minutes or until breadcrumbs are brown.

CHICKEN AND ALMOND SALAD

- 1 1/2 c. cooked chicken
- 3/4 c. diced celery
- 1 1/2 tbsp. lemon juice
- 1/2 c. seedless white grapes
- 1/2 c. almonds
- 1/2 tsp. dries mustard
- 3/4 tsp. salt
- 1/16 tsp. pepper
- 1/8 c. light cream
- 1 hardboiled egg, sliced
- 1/2 c. mayonnaise

Mix cream and mayonnaise together with mustard, lemon juice, salt and pepper. Pour over other ingredients. Delicious!

CHICKEN SALAD

- 1 can chicken, chopped (or 5 oz. cooked chicken)
- 1/2 c. chopped celery
- 1/3 c. chopped sweet pickle
- 1 boiled egg, chopped
- 1/2 c. salad dressing

CHICKEN SALAD SUPREME

- 2 lg. chickens (3 to 4 lb. each to make 6 to 8 c. cooked meat)
- 4 tbsp. salad oil
- 4 tbsp. orange juice
- 4 tbsp. vinegar
- 2 tsp. salt
- 3 c. mandarin oranges
- 2 c. pineapple chunks
- 3 c. green grapes
- Slivered almonds
- 3 c. diced celery
- 2 1/2 c. raw rice
- 1 qt. mayonnaise

Cut chicken into pieces and boil until tender with no seasonings. Remove skin and fat first. Remove meat from bones and cut into cubes. Mix together oil, orange juice, vinegar, salt, marinate chicken in this mixture in refrigerator overnight.

Drain fruit well, add to nuts and celery the next day; add to chicken mixture. Cook rice until tender in boiling water, drain, blanch with cold water, drain well; add to chicken mixture.

Add mayonnaise, mix well. Serve with crackers and lettuce or in pocket bread.

CHICKEN SOUP WITH TINY MEATBALLS

- 2 lb. stewing chicken
- 4 c. water
- 2 1/2 tsp. basil
- 1/2 lb. sm. onions
- 1 bay leaf
- 1 clove garlic
- 5 carrots, sliced
- Parsley and celery leaves

Place chicken in water in large saucepan. Add salt, pepper, basil, bay leaf and garlic. Bring to boil. Lower heat and simmer slowly for 1/2 hour or until chicken is tender. Remove chicken from pan. Cool and carefully skim fat from surface of soup.

Bring soup to a boil and add onions, carrots, parsley and celery, simmer gently for 10 minutes.

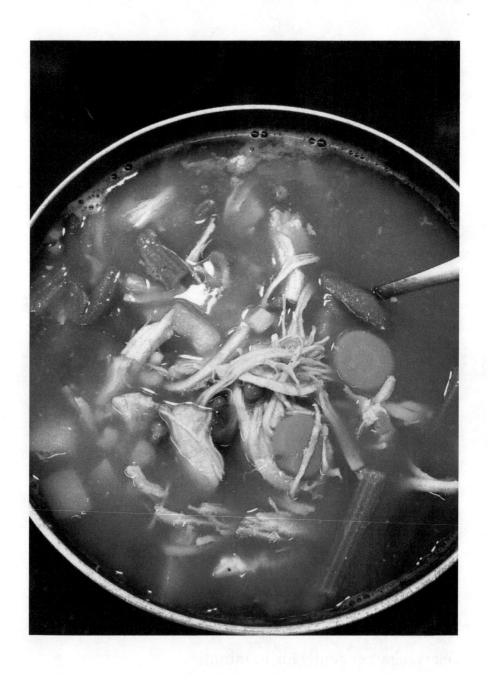

--MEATBALLs --

- 1 c. finely minced beef
- 1 egg
- 1 slice crumbly white bread
- 1/2 tsp. salt
- Freshly ground black pepper

Mix beef with egg, bread, salt and pepper. Form into small meatballs, add meatballs to soup and simmer for 35 minutes. Meanwhile, skin and bone the chicken.

Cut meat into small pieces. Garnish the soup with chicken and serve.

CHICKEN TORTELLINI SOUP

- 2 carrots
- 1 onion
- 2 garlic cloves
- 3 cans cream of chicken soup
- 6 c. water
- 1 tsp. oregano
- 1 tsp. basil
- 1 pkg. boneless chicken breasts, cut into bite-size pieces
- 1 bag cheese tortellini
- 2 boxes frozen broccoli

Cook chicken in small amount of oil. While meat cooks, chop vegetables and open cans. Add all above ingredients to large kettle except for the tortellini and frozen broccoli.

These 2 ingredients you add the last 10 minutes or so before serving so that they are not over cooked. Simmer the other ingredients for an hour or however long you like. Soup tastes great with freshly grated Italian cheese and a loaf of Italian or French bread.

SEASONING MIX FOR CHICKEN

- 2 1/2 tsp. salt
- 1 1/2 tsp. paprika
- 1 tsp. onion powder
- 3/4 tsp. savory
- 1/4 tsp. coriander
- 3/4 tsp. garlic powder
- 1/2 tsp. black pepper
- 1/2 tsp. thyme
- 1/2 tsp. basil, dried crushed sweet

Mix all ingredients well. Makes 2 tablespoons plus 2 teaspoons.

MARINADE FOR CHICKEN

- 1/2 c. shoyu
- 1/4 c. water
- 1/3 c. salad oil
- 2 tbsp. dried minced onion
- 2 tbsp. sesame seeds
- 1 tbsp. sugar
- 1 tsp. ground ginger
- 1/8 tsp. dried red pepper
- 3/4 tsp. garlic powder

Mix together all the above ingredients. Marinate chicken parts overnight, turning once, or twice to insure complete marinate.

Bake in 350-degree oven for 1 hour. If you intend to use a charcoal grill, bake in oven first for 45 minutes and on grill for 15 minutes. Place marinade in a Ziploc bag with chicken parts. This makes turning easier.

CHINESE CHICKEN SALAD DRESSING

- 2 tsp. sesame oil
- 2 tbsp. sesame seeds, roasted
- 2 tbsp. sugar
- 2 tbsp. mayonnaise
- 2 tbsp. lemon juice
- 2 tbsp. oil
- 2 tbsp. shoyu

Combine all ingredients and mix well. Drizzle over salad just before serving. This is also a good marinade to pour over skinned chicken the night before grilling it.

For the salad, prepare a green salad, with shredded cooked chicken. Sprinkle top with dry chow Mein noodles.

CHICKEN CASSEROLE

- 6 chicken breasts
- 2 onions
- 8 c. water (approximately)
- 3/4 loaf bread
- Celery
- Poultry seasoning
- 2 tbsp. melted butter
- 1 can cream of mushroom soup
- 1 can cream of chicken soup
- Sharp cheese, sliced

Boil chicken breasts with 1 onion in approximately 8 cups of water until tender. Remove skin and bones and separate into pieces. Save chicken stock. Use 13 x 9-inch pan (sprayed with Pam).

Tear small hunks of bread (about 3/4 of a loaf) and lay in bottom of pan. Slice 1 onion thin and lay on top of bread. Sprinkle celery, poultry seasoning on top.

Lay chicken pieces on top. Melt margarine and pour over chicken pieces. Combine mushroom soup, cream of chicken soup and pour on top. Cover the top with sharp cheese sliced all over the top. Bake until done.

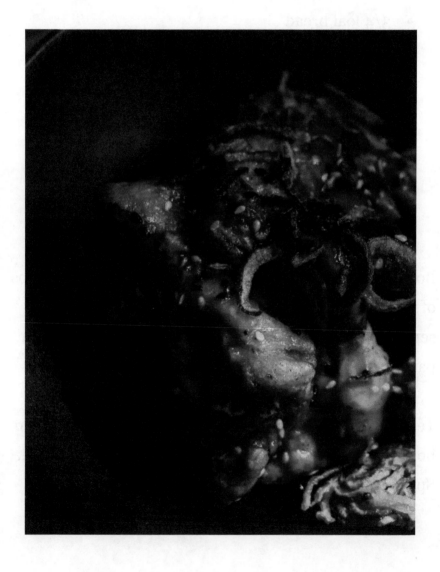

CHICKEN DIVAN

- 3 or 4 deboned chicken breasts
- 2 cans cream of chicken soup
- 1 tsp. lemon juice
- 1 c. sharp American cheese, shredded
- 2 (10 oz.) pkgs. frozen broccoli
- 1/2 c. soft breadcrumbs, mixed with 2 tsp. melted butter
- 1c. mayonnaise

Simmer chicken until tender. Cook broccoli in salted water, drain. Arrange broccoli in greased casserole dish. Place halved chicken breasts on top of broccoli. Combine soup, mayonnaise and lemon juice. Pour over chicken.

Sprinkle cheese and breadcrumbs on top. Bake at 350 degrees for 25 minutes. Prepare rice or potatoes for 6 people and serve.

CHICKEN DIVAN

- 1 lb. cooked chicken, no bones
- 1/2 lb. cooked chopped broccoli
- 1 c. shredded extra sharp cheddar cheese
- 1 can cream of mushroom soup
- 1 c. croutons

Preheat oven to 350 degrees. Mix chicken (bite-size pieces), broccoli, cheese and soup together. Pour into 8 x 11-inch casserole dish. Place croutons on top.

Bake at 350 degrees for 1/2 hour or until hot. Serves 6.

CHICKEN POT PIE

- 3 lb. chicken
- 1 can French onion soup
- 1 lg. carrot
- 1 lg. celery
- Flour to thicken gravy
- Water
- 1 double crust

Preheat oven to 400 degrees. Simmer whole chicken in water with carrot and celery until done, 1 1/2 to 2 hours. Pick meat off and cut into bite-size pieces. Refrigerate chicken and broth separately overnight.

Next day, remove fat from broth as well as carrots and celery. Add onion soup and bring to boil. Thicken gravy with flour-water paste. Strain gravy to remove onions.

Put chicken in bottom crust. Pour gravy on top. Place top crust and bake at 400 degrees for 30 minutes.

CHICKEN WITH RICE

- 3 to 3 1/2 lbs. chicken, cut into serving pieces
- 1/4 c. butter or margarine
- 1 1/2 c. instant rice
- 1 (10 1/2 oz.) can condensed cream of chicken soup
- 1c. water
- 1 tsp. instant chicken bouillon crystals or 1 chicken bouillon cube

Preheat skillet (medium heat), uncovered. Add butter or margarine and allow to melt. Place chicken pieces into skillet and brown on both sides. Season with salt and pepper. Remove chicken from skillet.

Reduce heat to "simmer" and add rice. Combine soup, water and bouillon. Pour 1/2 mixture over rice. Replace chicken pieces into skillet onto rice. Pour remaining soup mixture over chicken.

Cover and simmer, 35 to 40 minutes or until chicken is done. Makes 4 to 6 servings.

CHICKEN TIKKA

- 5/8 c. yogurt
- 4 crushed garlic cloves
- 1 1/2 inch fresh ginger, peeled & chopped
- 1 sm. onion, grated
- 1 1/2 tsp. chili powder
- 1 tbsp. ground coriander
- 1 tsp. salt
- 4 chicken breasts, skinned & boned
- 1 lg. onion, thinly sliced into rings
- 2 lg. tomatoes, sliced
- 2 tbsp. coriander leaves

Combine first 7 ingredients and set aside. Cut chicken into 1-inch cubes. Add to marinade, mix well, cover and chill for 6 hours or overnight. Heat broiler.

Put chicken on skewers or in broiler pan and broil (or grill) 5 to 8 minutes, turning occasionally until cooked through. Garnish with onion rings, tomatoes, and coriander leaves and serve. 4 servings.

HONEY SPICED CAJUN CHICKEN

- Paul Prudhomynes seafood magic
- 10 oz. pounded chicken breast
- Cooked linguini
- 3 sliced mushrooms
- 1 diced tomato
- 2 tbsp. mustard
- 4 tbsp. honey
- 3 oz. cream

Pat the chicken in the seasonings, then in a very hot fry pan; sear the chicken on both sides until it is done.

Take chicken, slice, put back in pan with a little oil, the diced tomato and mushrooms for 2 minutes.

Add the honey, mustard and cream. Cook for 5 minutes at medium heat. toss in linguini. Serves 2.

ITALIAN CHICKEN

- 2/3 c. flour
- 1 tsp. salt
- 1/2 c. vegetable oil
- 1 green pepper
- 1/2 tsp. pepper
- 1/2 tsp. garlic salt
- Sliced onion
- 1 lg. jar spaghetti sauce
- Chicken (boneless) breasts, quartered

Wash chicken. Mix flour, salt, pepper and garlic together. Coat chicken, brown in oil, then drain.

Top chicken with peppers and onions (sliced). Add sauce on top. Cover and simmer about 1 hour. Serve with spaghetti.

LEMON - PARSLEY CHICKEN BREASTS

- 2 whole chicken breasts, boned & skinned
- 1/3 c. white wine
- 1/3 c. lemon juice
- 2 cloves fresh minced garlic
- 3 tbsp. breadcrumbs
- 2 tbsp. olive oil
- 1/4 c. parsley, fresh

In a measuring cup, combine wine, lemon juice and garlic. Pound each breast until ¼ inch thick and lightly coat with breadcrumbs. Heat olive oil in a large skillet and brown chicken, 5 minutes on each side.

Stir wine mixture and pour over chicken in skillet. Sprinkle on parsley and let simmer 5 minutes. Serve with pan juices.

MARY'S CHICKEN DISH

- 6 pieces boneless breast of chicken
- 4 tbsp. olive oil
- 2 tbsp. butter
- 1 clove garlic
- Breadcrumbs
- 2 eggs
- 1 bouillon cube
- 1 can chicken broth
- 6 slices of Mozzarella cheese

Dip boneless, skinless chicken breast in breadcrumbs and eggs. In a large skillet, heat olive oil, butter, garlic and melt bouillon cube. Make sure to put heat on low so oil does not burn.

When oil is hot, brown chicken on both sides in oil, increase heat so chicken gets nice and brown on both sides, lower heat and add chicken broth.

Simmer until hot. Add Mozzarella cheese to top chicken.

NO - PEEK SKILLET CHICKEN

- 2 tbsp. olive or vegetable oil
- 2 1/2 to 3 lb. chicken, cut into serving pieces
- 1 (14 oz.) can whole tomatoes, peeled, undrained 1
- (4 1/2 oz.) jar sliced mushrooms, drained
- 1 garlic clove, minced
- 1 env. Lipton Recipe Secrets onion soup mix
- Hot cooked noodles

In a 12-inch skillet, heat oil and brown the chicken; drain. Stir in tomatoes, mushrooms and garlic combined with soup mix.

Simmer covered for 45 minutes or until chicken is tender. Serve, if desired, over hot noodles.

*Lipton Recipe Secrets beef mushroom soup mix would be a delicious substitute in this recipe.

QUICK CHICKEN

- 1 can cream of mushroom soup
- 1 can cream of chicken soup
- 1 c. milk
- 5 lbs. cut up cooked chicken
- 1 pt. sour cream
- 1 pkg. Pepperidge Farm stuffing mix

Mix soups, sour cream and milk. Add chicken. Mix all ingredients and layer in baking dish alternating with stuffing mix. Bake at 350 degrees for 1 hour.

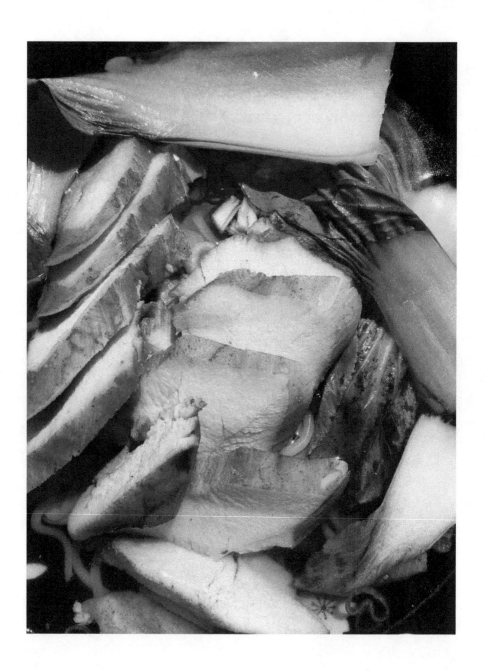

SWEET & SOUR CHICKEN

- 1 frying chicken, cut up
- 1 tbsp. melted butter
- Dash of salt, pepper, ginger
- 3 celery stalks
- 1 can pineapple (chunk)
- 2 tbsp. brown sugar
- 3 tbsp. water
- 1 1/2 tbsp. soy sauce
- 1 tbsp. vinegar
- 1 tbsp. cornstarch
- 1 red pepper (optional)

Rinse chicken, place skin side up in oiled pan. Pour melted butter over chicken. Sprinkle chicken with salt, pepper, ginger, diced celery. Bake chicken at 325 degrees for about 20 minutes. Drain pineapple juice into cup.

Blend in brown sugar, water, soy sauce, vinegar, cornstarch. Pour mixture over chicken in pan. Top with pineapple chunks and pepper.

CHICKEN CACCIATORE

- 1 pkg. chicken
- 1/4 c. butter
- 1/2 c. sherry
- 15 oz. can stewed tomato bits
- 1 (6 oz.) can mushrooms
- 1 pkg. Italian dressing mix
- 1/4 c. chopped green pepper
- 1 tsp. Italian seasoning
- Garlic powder, to taste
- Bayleaf

Boil chicken until done. Save water (use this to boil rice in). Cut chicken into tiny squares. Brown in butter and sherry.

Add tomatoes, mushrooms, Italian dressing mix, green pepper and other seasonings.

Bring to boil and simmer for one hour. Serve over rice.

SUNDAY FRIED CHICKEN

- 1 whole chicken or any combo of chicken pieces
- 1 to 2 c. of flour for coating
- Salt and pepper to taste
- 4 tbsp. butter
- 4 tbsp. Crisco
- 2 beaten eggs

Wash and dry chicken parts. Combine salt, pepper, and flour and coat chicken. Dip each piece in egg mixture and brown each side in hot, melted shortening and butter.

Lower heat and cook for about 15 minutes more on each side. Use heavy iron or aluminum frypan if possible.

Remove from pan and drain on paper towels. Pour all but 3 tablespoons of fat from pan and return to heat.

Add 3 tablespoons flour to pan and stir with fat until lightly browned.

Add 2 cups of milk and some parsley or parsley flakes and cook on medium heat until thick. Put in gravy boat and serve with the chicken that you have arranged on a platter.

HONEY BAKED CHICKEN

- 3 or 4 lbs. chicken, cut up
- 1/2 c. margarine, melted
- 1/2 c. honey
- 1 tsp. salt
- 1/4 c. prep. mustard
- 1 tsp. curry

Pour over chicken. Bake at 350 degrees for 1 1/4 hours.
Basting every 15 minutes.

BAKED CHICKEN

- 1/2 c. ketchup
- 1/2 c. mayonnaise
- 3 tbsp. minced onion
- Breadcrumbs or crushed corn flakes
- 2 to 2 1/2 cut up chicken

Mix first three ingredients and dip chicken. Coat with crumbs or flakes. Bake on greased pan or roll lined pan.

Bake at 375 degrees for 40 to 45 minutes.

BAKED CHICKEN BREASTS

- 8 chicken breast halves, skinned
- 8 slices Swiss cheese
- 1 can cream of chicken soup
- 1/3 c. white wine
- 1 c. Pepperidge herb stuffing mix
- 1/4 tsp. melted butter or margarine

Put chicken in very lightly greased baking dish. Top with cheese. Combine soup and wine. Spoon over chicken.

Sprinkle with stuffing. Drizzle melted butter over chicken. Bake at 350 degrees 45 to 50 minutes. Serves 6 to 8.

SICILIAN CHICKEN

- 1 tbsp. plus 1 tbsp. saffron ace
- 1 lg. onion, sliced
- 1 lg. green pepper, sliced
- 1/2 c. fresh mush berries, sliced
- 1 1/2 lbs. boneless chicken cubed
- 18 oz. can tomato sauce
- 16 oz. tomatoes, chopped drained
- 1 tsp. Worcestershire sauce
- 1 tsp. oregano
- 1/2 tsp. basil
- 1/4 tsp. garlic powder
- Lite salt and pepper to taste

Heat oil in large nonstick skillet. Add onions green pepper and mushrooms. Cook until slightly tender. Add chicken. Cook, turning chicken frequently until pinkness is gone. Add remaining ingredients.

Cover and simmer for 5 to 10 minutes until heated through. Serve over rice. Makes 4 servings (1 protein, 2 vegetables per serving).

ROAST CHICKEN WITH ALMONDS

- 10 chicken breast halves
- Salt and pepper
- 1 (5 1/2 oz.) pkg. slivered almonds
- 1 (10 1/2 oz.) can cream of mushroom soup
- 1 (10 1/2 oz.) can cream of chicken soup
- 1/4 to 1/2 c. dry white wine, or water or other liquid
- Parmesan cheese

Spread chicken in very lightly greased baking dish. Cover with 2/3 of the almonds. Mix soups with wine. Pour over chicken and almonds.

Sprinkle Parmesan cheese on top and then sprinkle remaining almonds over. Bake at 350 degrees for 2 hours uncovered. Serves 8 to 10.

WALDORF CHICKEN

- 6 chicken breasts, boned and skinned
- 1 c. unsweetened apple juice
- 1/4 tsp. ground ginger
- 1 tbsp. cornstarch
- 2 c. unpared red apples, chopped
- 2 stalks celery, sliced
- 3 tbsp. raisins
- 1 tbsp. sliced green onion
- 1 tbsp. lemon juice
- 1/4 tsp. salt, opt.

Place chicken, 1/2 cup apple juice, and lemon juice, salt and pepper in nonstick skillet. Heat to boiling, cover and simmer for 20 minutes or until chicken is tender and done. Remove chicken.

Mix remaining apple juice and cornstarch. Stirring constantly. Add remaining ingredients. Arrange chicken on plate. Top with sauce.